best of the CORRS

Wise Publications
London / New York / Paris / Sydney / Copenhagen / Madrid / Tokyo

Exclusive distributors:
Music Sales Limited, 8/9 Frith Street, London W1B 3JB, England.
Music Sales Pty Limited, 120 Rothschild Avenue, Rosebery, NSW 2018, Australia.

Order No. AM973412
ISBN 0-7119-9253-3
This book © Copyright 2001 by Wise Publications.

Music arrangements by Derek Jones.
Music processed by Paul Ewers Music Design.
Artwork courtesy of Atlantic Records.

Printed and bound in the United Kingdom.

Your Guarantee of Quality:
As publishers, we strive to produce every book to the highest commercial standards.
While endeavouring to retain the original running order of the recorded album,
the book has been carefully designed to minimise awkward page turns and to make
playing from it a real pleasure.
Particular care has been given to specifying acid-free, neutral-sized paper made from
pulps which have not been elemental chlorine bleached.
This pulp is from farmed sustainable forests and was produced with special regard
for the environment. Throughout, the printing and binding have been planned to ensure
a sturdy, attractive publication which should give years of enjoyment.
If your copy fails to meet our high standards, please inform us and we will gladly
replace it.

Music Sales' complete catalogue describes thousands of titles and is available
in full colour sections by subject, direct from Music Sales Limited.
Please state your areas of interest and send a cheque/postal order for £1.50
for postage to: Music Sales Limited, Newmarket Road, Bury St. Edmunds,
Suffolk IP33 3YB.

www.musicsales.com

WOULD YOU BE HAPPIER?

Words & Music by Andrea Corr, Caroline Corr, Sharon Corr & Jim Corr

12

Verse 2:
Are you not afraid to tell your story now
But everyone is gone, it's too late
Why is everything you've ever said or done
Not the way you planned, mistake
And so you promised that tomorrow
Be different than today.

Would you be happier *etc.*

SO YOUNG

Words & Music by Andrea Corr, Caroline Corr, Sharon Corr & Jim Corr

Verse 2:
We are chasing the moon
Just running wild and free,
We are following through
Every dream and every need.

'Cause we are so young now *etc.*

Runaway

Words & Music by Andrea Corr, Caroline Corr, Sharon Corr & Jim Corr

1. Say it's true,   there's no-thing like⸺ me and you.
(Verse 2 see block lyric)

20

Repeat ad lib. to fade

Verse 2:
Close the door, lay down upon the floor
And by candlelight make love to me through the night
Cos I have runaway
I have runaway, yeah, yeah
I have runaway, runaway
I have runaway with you.

Cos I have fallen in love, *etc.*

BREATHLESS

Words & Music by R.J. Lange, Andrea Corr, Caroline Corr, Sharon Corr & Jim Corr

1. The day-light's fad - ing slow - ly,___
(Verse 2 see block lyric)

but time___ with you___ is stand - ing still. I'm wait - ing for___

___ you on - ly,___ the slight - est touch___ and I___ feel weak.___

I can - not lie,___ from you___ I___ can - not hide.

And I'm los - ing the will____ to___ try.____

D.%. (I've lost____ my____)

Can't hide____ it, can't fight____ it. So____

go____ on, go____ on,____ come on, leave me breath - less.____

Tempt____ me, tease____ me____ un - til I can't de - ny____ this

Verse 2:
And if there's no tomorrow
And all we have is here and now
I'm happy just to have you
You're all the love I need somehow
It's like a dream
Although I'm not asleep
And I never want to wake up
Don't lose it, don't leave it.

So go on, go on *etc.*

RADIO

Words & Music by Andrea Corr, Caroline Corr, Sharon Corr & Jim Corr

late at night and I'm feel-ing down, there are cou-ples stand-ing on the street shar-in'

(Verse 2 see block lyric)

But you are in my head, swim-ing for-ev-er in my head, tang-led in my dreams, swim - ming for-ev-er.

So I lis-ten to the ra-di-o, and all the songs we used to know,

ra - di - o,____ re - mem - ber how we used to go.____

You____

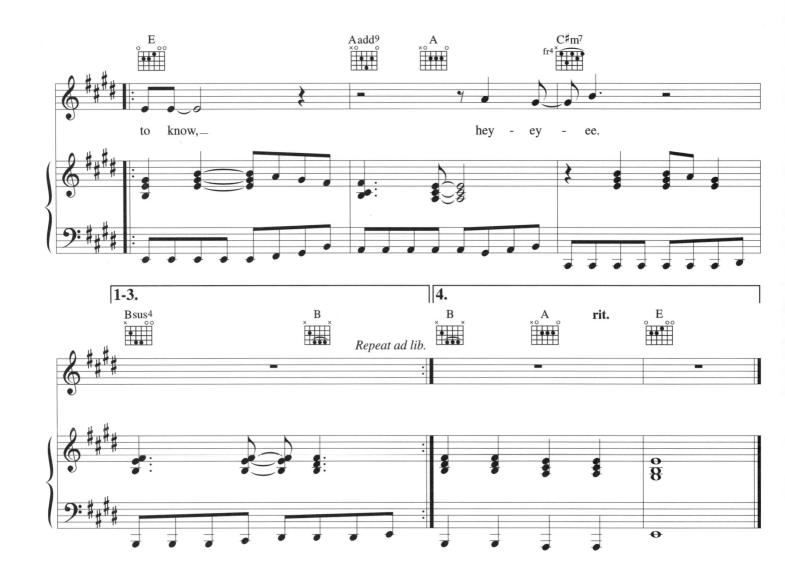

to know,—   hey - ey - ee.

1-3.   **4.**

Repeat ad lib.

Verse 2:

Now it's morning light and it's cold outside
Caught up in a distant dream
I turn and think that you are by my side
So I leave my bed and I try to dress
Wondering why my mind plays tricks
And fools me in to thinking you are there
But you're just in my head
Swimming forever in my head
Not lying in my bed
Just swimming forever.

So listen to the radio *etc*.

WHAT CAN I DO

Words & Music by Andrea Corr, Caroline Corr, Sharon Corr & Jim Corr

1. I have-n't slept at all in days;
(Verse 3 see block lyric)

It's been so long since we have talked.

Verse 3:
Maybe there's nothing more to say;
And, in a funny way, I'm calm.
Because the power is not mine,
I'm just gonna let it fly.

THE RIGHT TIME

Words & Music by Andrea Corr, Caroline Corr, Sharon Corr & Jim Corr

Verse 3:
Keep it going, let's not lose it, feel the flow
Oh, flying free in a fantasy, with you I'll go.

This is the right time, *etc.*

I NEVER LOVED YOU ANYWAY

Words & Music by Andrea Corr, Caroline Corr, Sharon Corr, Jim Corr & Carole Bayer Sager

1. You bored me with your stories,—
(Verse 2 see block lyric)
I can't be-lieve that I en--dured you for as long as I did.—— I'm hap-py it's ov-er,

Yeah, I am.

And when you go— I will— re - mem - ber I must re -

no, I did-n't love you an-y-way,___ nev-er tru-ly loved you

loved you an-y-way,___ nev-er loved you an-y-

an-y-way.___ I'm so hap-py you're mov-ing a-way,___

way, I nev-er loved you an-y-way.___

yeah, I'm de-light-ed you're mov-ing a-way.___

Repeat to fade

Verse 2:
Valentino, I don't think so
You watching MTV while I lie dreaming in an empty bed.
And come to think of it, I was misled
My flat, my food, my everything and thoughts inside my head.

Before you go I must remember
To have a quiet word with that girl.
Does she know you're not a spender?
Well I just have to say.

I never really *etc.*

IRRESISTIBLE

Words & Music by R.J. Lange, Andrea Corr, Caroline Corr, Sharon Corr & Jim Corr

Now you feel what I'm feel - ing.—   Don't you know that it's more?—
(Don't you feel what I'm feel - ing.)

Verse 2:
So can't you see I'm tortured
Oh can't you hear my pain
If you just let me show you
I'll be your summer rain
Then you'll feel that you want me
(The way I'm feeling)
Just like I want you
(The way I want you)
And you'll know nothing's better
It's like nothing before.

You're irresistible *etc.*

FORGIVEN, NOT FORGOTTEN

Words & Music by Andrea Corr, Caroline Corr, Sharon Corr & Jim Corr

1. All a - lone,___ star - ing on,___ watch-ing her life go___ by.___
(Verse 2 see block lyric)

___ When her days are grey and her nights are black,

diff - er - ent___ shades of mun - dane,___ and the one-eyed fur - ry toy___ that

lies up - on the bed has of - ten heard___ her cry___ and heard her

Still a - lone,_____ star - ing on,_____

Bodhrán

70

Verse 2:
A bleeding heart torn apart
Left on an icy grave
And a room where they once lay
Face to face
Nothing could get in their way
But now the memories of the man
Are haunting her days
And the craving never fades
She's still dreaming of a man.
Long forgiven
But not forgotten.

You're forgiven *etc.*

LOUGH ERIN SHORE

Traditional, arranged by Andrea Corr, Caroline Corr, Sharon Corr & Jim Corr

ONLY WHEN I SLEEP

Words & Music by Andrea Corr, Caroline Corr, Sharon Corr, Jim Corr,
John Shanks, Paul Peterson & Oliver Leiber

It's reach-ing through my skin, mov-ing from with-in, and clutch-es at my breast. yeah But it's on-ly when I

Verse 2:
And when I wake from slumber
Your shadow's disappeared
Your breath is just a sea mist
Surrounding my body.
I'm working through the daytime
But when it's time to rest
I'm lying in my bed
Listening to my breath
Falling from the edge.

LOVE TO LOVE YOU

Words & Music by Andrea Corr, Caroline Corr, Sharon Corr & Jim Corr

Repeat ad lib. to fade

Break— those pil - lars down.—

Verse 2:
You recognised my barrier to love
I know there's nothing worse than unrequited love, (unrequited)
So I prayed to God that I could give the love you gave to me
But something's lying in my way, preventing it to be.

(Though you should leave me)
Time make it be alright
(Though you must leave me)
Believe me when I tell you

I would love to love you like you do me *etc.*

All The Love In The World

Words & Music by R.J. Lange, Andrea Corr, Caroline Corr, Sharon Corr & Jim Corr

1. I'm not look-ing for some-one to talk— to. I've got my friends, I'm
(Verse 2 see block lyric)

Verse 2:
I've often wondered if love's an illusion
Just to get you through the loneliest days
I can't criticize it, I have no hesitation
My imagination just stole me away
Still I believe I'm missing something real
I need someone who really sees me.

Don't wanna wake up alone *etc.*

EVERYBODY HURTS

Words & Music by Peter Buck, Bill Berry, Mike Mills & Michael Stipe

1. When your day is long_____ and the
(Verse 2 & 3 see block lyrics)

night, and the night is yours a - lone,_____

Verse 2:
When your day is night, hold on, hold on
If you feel like letting go, hold on
If you're sure you've had too much of this life, hang on
'Cause everybody hurts, sometimes
Take comfort in your friends
Everybody hurts.

Verse 3:
If you're on your own in this life
And the days and nights are long
If you're sure you've had too much of this life, to hang on
Everybody hurts sometimes
Everybody cries sometimes
Everybody hurts sometimes.

Give Me A Reason

Words & Music by Andrea Corr, Caroline Corr, Sharon Corr & Jim Corr

Verse 2:
You'll never know the love I felt
Wanting, waiting for you
It takes a weak heart to forget
Follow, follow it through.

Now my body's weak etc.

DREAMS

Words & Music by Stevie Nicks

Verse 2:
Now here I go again I see the crystal vision
But I keep my visions to myself
Well it's only me who wants to wrap around your dreams
And have you any dreams you'd like to sell?
Dreams of loneliness.

Like a heartbeat *etc.*

MAKE YOU MINE

Words & Music by Andrea Corr, Caroline Corr, Sharon Corr, Jim Corr & David Foster

day - light_ takes_ you_ I'll miss you_ till you come back_ home to_

1.

_ me and I can make_ you mine._ Oh yeah,_

2.

oh_ yeah._ _ me. When you come back_ home to_

_ me, I'll break you, I'll chase_ you. You'll find_

Verse 2:
Wanting you
Every waking moment I'm on fire
Always needing you
I'm aching for you only I'll never tire
Promise me this is how we'll be
I'm falling deeper every day.

But when the night turns over *etc.*

THE CORRS

SOLO present

THE CORRS

The Shepherds Bush Empire

Tuesday 2nd December 1997
Doors 7:00pm/Showtime 7:30pm
£12.50 in Advance

NO SMOKING

LEVEL 1
UNRESERVED SEATING/STANDING

1424

Irish quartet **The Corrs** return to the UK in March for a ten date headlining tour. The stint will include a show at the Royal Albert Hall on St Patrick's Day (March 17th) which will be broadcast on BBC1 that evening. The brother and three sisters from County Louth shot to worldwide stage with the release of their debut album 'Forgiven Not Forgotten', which went gold or platinum in the UK, across Europe, in Australia, New Zealand and Canada. 'Talk On Corners', featuring new single 'What Can I Do To Make You Love Me' released on March 16th, is set to consolidate on that success. The full list of their dates is as follows:

March 12th St. David's Hall **Cardiff**, 13th The Barbican Centre **York** 14th The Apollo **Manchester**, 16th Symphony Hall **Birmingham**, 17th The Royal Albert Hall **London**, 18th The Royal Concert Hall **Nottingham**, 20th The Royal Concert Hall **Glasgow**, 22nd City Hall **Sheffield**, 23rd Dearngate **Northampton**, 24th Fairfield Hall **Croydon**.

He's Not Bitter

INHALT
FILES: THE CORRS, NADINE NORELL, RELEASES
TV-DATES, NEW RELEASES, TOUR-SCHEDULE

LEADH
Y PARK, LONDON
Y 10th JUNE 2000
TAGE
MAIN
DUCTION
ARENA
CORRS

THE CORRS

Martes
4 de Junio
(Madrid)

No. 00101

El Sol
C/ Jardines 3

SOUNDCHECK 4.0
DOORS 6.00

THE CORRS
7.30-8.15

INVITACION Prohibida su venta
ESTA ENTRADA SUPONE LA ACEPTACION DE LAS CONDICIONES DETALLADAS AL DORSO

[THE CORRS]
KARSTEN JAHNKE
KONZERTDIREKTION GMBH, HAMBURG

7/7
ALL AREAS

THE CORRS
WORLD 97/98 TOUR
ACCESS ALL AREAS

Aftershow
eas

VIP

FORT LAUDERDALE 24/4/0

Tuesday
14th May
1996
Doors

THE CORRS

EMPIRE
SOLO-TTG Present

MCD OLIVER BARRY PRESENT
THE CORRS
LANSDOWNE ROAD
GATES OPEN AT 7.00PM
TUNE TO 2FM FOR DETAILS
SAT 17-JUL-99
LOWER T
ROW 19 SEAT 118
YELLOW ROUTE

ARTIST
MEDIA AREA

9. HASTE TO THE W
10. SECRET LIFE
11. ON YOUR OWN
12. SOMEDAY
13. LOUGH ERIN SHO
14. LOVE TO LOVE
15. TOSS THE FEATH

VENUE
DATE